Raymond Waites

FESTIVE TABLES

Photographs by Tom McCavera

A Bulfinch Press Book   Little, Brown and Company   Boston • Toronto • London

To the friends
who have shared
my table
and made my
golden memories.

———

To Tom McCavera,
my photographer,
for his great talent
and endless support.

———

To Rita Sue Siegel,
for her tireless efforts
and good friendship.

———

To Cora Marcus,
for her bright spirit,
constant encouragement
and beautiful
eye.

My thanks to Bruce Bordelon, my lawyer,
for his advice and making my homes a reality
without which this book would not be possible.

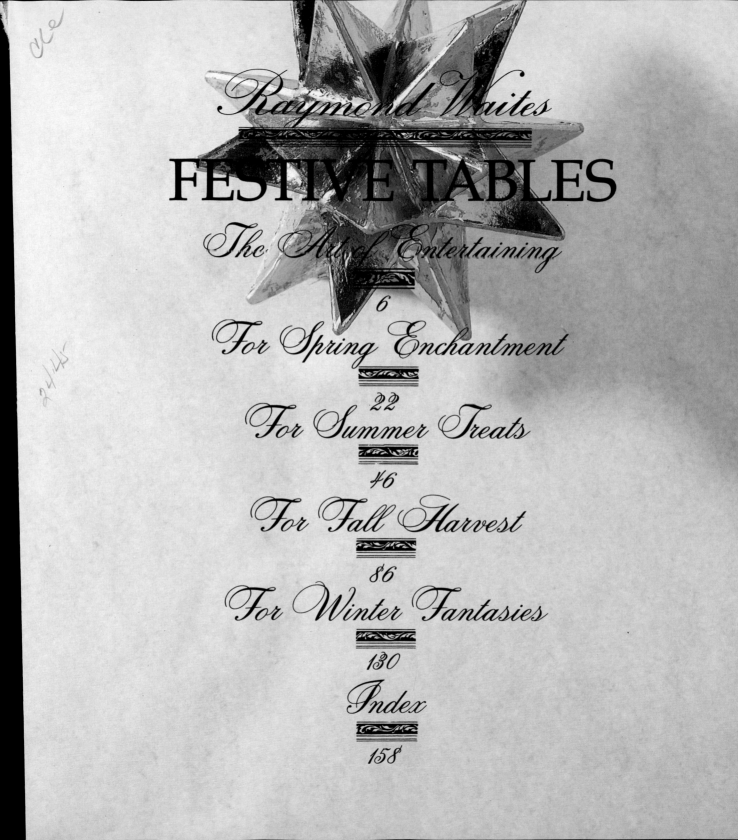

Raymond Waites

FESTIVE TABLES

The Art of Entertaining

FESTIVE TABLES

The Art of Entertaining

Entertaining is sharing. Sharing your affection, your creativity, your talents, and your home with your friends, both personal and professional. My book is about the joyful experience of making every table festive, every occasion a special one. Entertaining uses all the senses: sight, sound, taste, smell, and touch. A great evening happens when all of these things come together in magical ways. Many books have been written about the art of hospitality. Most deal only with the sense of taste. I believe that food is one of life's great joys, but a meal of sumptuous flavors that is not visually pleasing is not festive. This book, *Festive Tables*, is about using all the senses, because even the simplest menu done with grand gesture can be a night to be remembered for a lifetime.

My wife, Nancy Candler Waites, and I live hectic, fast-paced, urban lives. We're both Southerners brought up in a tradition of elegant, formal dining. Even in modest Southern households, a tradition of Sunday dinners set with white linen, silver, and gracious foods shared with family was a way of life.

A new casual attitude is evolving. The eighteenth-century silver plate fish knife is perfect for this nontraditional presentation. Fish knives aren't only for fish. They are beautiful, so use them when it makes you happy.

GOAT CHEESE WITH HERBS

Serves 6
Ingredients:
12-oz. mild goat cheese in a log
1 cup olive oil
2 tablespoons cracked whole black pepper
2 tablespoons oregano
2 tablespoons dried sweet basil leaf
1 tablespoon dried tarragon
1 tablespoon Crab Boil
3 slices bread toasted

1. Cut goat cheese into six patties.
2. Layer into jam jar.
3. Mix all other ingredients into olive oil.
4. Pour over goat cheese. Cover.
5. Refrigerate. To serve, bring to room temperature and provide toast.

The traditional Finnish kitchen is full of antique elements of Finnish entertaining. Russian samovars, carved wooden molds. Finnish ceramics, and a sheaf of wheat. Armi Ratia, founder of Marimekko, my mentor, created magical, festive tables at Bokars, her country house, that inspired me.

*M*y favorite accent color is the luscious, opulent sheen of gold. And nothing but candlelight gilds an evening even more. From my collection of table objects (from left), an enchanting golden rabbit, golden doilies, a golden teapot, a garland of gilded brown paper, a collection of gilded forks, gilded acorn napkin rings, gilded asparagus, a mirror-inlaid pot and plastic fruit objects, a collection of fruited napkin rings, and a gold-banded terra-cotta service plate.

Auburn University is where Nancy and I met and fell in love, then we moved to New York to study at Pratt Institute. From our earliest days, we had friends over for our down-home Southern fare. As our professional lives became more demanding in time and energy, it would have been easy to forsake our love of entertaining. Instead, we simplified the process,

concentrating on maximum effect for minimum effort. It is not unusual for us to have people over on the spur of the moment. To make this a

joy and not drudgery, we've created magical tricks to have an evening be wonderful and inventive without hours of labor.

Creating festive tables for your friends is an opportunity to remove yourself from your everyday world. Our modern world is hectic, full of stress, even danger-

ous, but in your own home you can invent your own world. It's the one place you can control all the elements and create your own feelings, aesthetic, and good times. Creating your home is truly one of life's great joys. I think of a home as an artist thinks of a blank canvas. An artist paints with color, texture, and light. His tools are canvas, brush, and pigment. In the same way, a home is created by the use of fabrics, furniture, colors, decorative arts, food, light, and music. By the way we layer these elements around us, we create our stage.

As we head toward the millennium, we're finding a need in ourselves to bring these beautiful treasures and traditions from our past into our lives again, though in a different way. We are like Janus, the Roman god that looks back as well as forward. We are bringing wonderful, elegant pieces into our lives but using them less formally than earlier generations. Now an elaborate silver candelabra can sit on a rustic, pine country table. Ethnic treasures we have collected from the markets of the world, like Moroccan bowls, sit next to fine English flatware. A personal style is made from the loves and dreams of each household.

There is not only a new aesthetic evolving but also a new etiquette; a new way of doing things molded by our times, and our finances.

Earlier in our nation's history, at church suppers, camp meetings, and even funerals, food was shared. A community spirit removed the financial burden from any one member. Today this type of shared energy and creativity can add a festive spirit and relieve the burden on the working couple.

Entertaining should be a joy, and food is one of life's great pleasures. These two simple facts explain why Nancy and I entertain frequently. Our guests, both business associates and friends, are, for the most part, discriminating, stylish people. It astounds me how the few recipes we've learned can be used throughout the year to enchant them. Chili (page 72), an old favorite, can become the centerpiece of many a festive time. It doesn't take a Ph.D. or a Cordon Bleu chef to make marvelous dinners for friends. With a handbook of a few personal favorites, you can create your own style, and your friends will look forward to sharing your home and your favorite recipes from year to year. Friends always ask for and are disappointed if Nancy's Kashmir Cream (page 84) is not served. It is a simple but outstanding dessert that takes less than fifteen minutes to prepare. Only three or four ingredients are combined, but these ingredients come together in such a special way that people ask for it again and again.

We collect recipes the way we collect our treasured objects. They are part of our home and a part of our life.

The limited palette of recipes and magical entertaining tricks in this book will dispel any fear of entertaining and give you the joyful experience of sharing your home with your friends.

The quickest and healthiest of hors d'oeuvres or desserts is fruit, here presented on a modern, overscaled majolica tray. So simple to arrange on a bed of Cranberry Dream Sauce (page 44). Garnish with endive leaves and sectioned plums. Serve on majolica plates with sugar or salt to taste from a cellar made from a gilded shell.

This book is about using the shortcuts but presenting the results in grand style. Over a lifetime, Nancy and I have built a treasure trove of decorative elements. We've made many of them. Others we have unearthed in antique fairs and flea markets, some were gifts from friends, and a treasured few were investments. Layered together, they are the tools of our entertaining. Learn to look around you. See what's in your cupboard and make use of the wonderful things you find.

*T*hroughout this book, you'll see how the colors of nature and the seasons become a natural extension of your entertaining. In the spring, the earth renews itself. Coming out of the gray days, the first crocuses and the fresh buds of green signal a rebirth, a freshness, a lightness of heart. Spring is a time of yellow: daffodils, tulips, and forsythia. Summer envelopes us with a warm sun. The pool area becomes our living room and the center of our summer entertaining. As Indian summer enfolds us in those last warm days we take advantage of the harvest season and make use of the sun's golden glow by spending time outdoors under the trees.

In New York fall is sig-

As friends return to the house in late afternoon from the beach or antique fairs, Nancy and I set a table with a variety of tortilla chips and salsas for our guests. We offer a simple wine and a choice of exotic beers as accompaniments. I use two sectioned eighteenth-century serving vessels for the various chips. Salsas are presented in Finnish bowls. Terra-cotta plates are stacked in baskets. The table decoration has been concocted from a flea market find of a feathered woman's hat filled with wooden and gilded fruit.

naled for us not only by the changing of flora and quality of light, but by the level of activity that returns to the city. You can feel the creative energy in the air from the increased activity in the theater, the art world, and the business world.

For our family, winter is the time of true fantasy. The holiday season envelops us with familiar themes, moods, foods, and flora. Our fantasies bloom in this most festive time of year. It may be cold, bustling, hectic, and stressful in the outside world, but in our homes we can create an atmosphere of warmth, friendship, shared times, and magical fantasy.

The year's finale comes in winter with our black-tie, formal fantasy. Each year, friends join us for a Christmas potluck dinner on December 19, our wedding anniversary. The gathering has grown to as many as 100 friends, a special evening of diverse food fantasies.

GOAT CHEESE AND HERB PIZZA

Serves 6–8
Ingredients:
1 12" frozen pizza shell, thawed
2 patties Parisian Goat Cheese with Herbs
1 large tomato, sliced
1½ cups shredded mozzarella cheese
1 clove garlic, peeled and finely chopped
cracked black pepper to taste
1 cup fresh parsley, coarsely chopped

1. Preheat oven to 450°.
2. Spread goat cheese over pizza shell.
3. Place tomato slices over cheese.
4. Cover tomatoes with shredded mozzarella.
5. Sprinkle with garlic and pepper.
6. Place in oven and bake for 20 minutes until cheese melts and crust browns.
7. Remove from oven. While cheese is still bubbling, garnish with parsley.
8. Cut and serve.

A simple presentation of gilded brown paper encircles Goat Cheese and Herb Pizzas creating a festive mood.

FESTIVE TABLES

For Spring Enchantment

Frische für die Sommertage

TEXT: VERA GRAAF · FOTOS: JON JENSEN

Paßt feines Altes zu vulgär Neuem, ja schrill Verplüschtem?
Keine Frage für Raymond Waites. Der amerikanische Einrichtungs-
Profi zieht seinem Haus einmal im Jahr ein neues
„Gewand" an, das er aus unterschiedlichen Objekten kreiert

30

After winter's gray cold, the spring renews us. Nancy and I return to East Hampton at the sign of the first crocus at our house. After a season in New York, the light and the spirit of spring refresh us. Our urban friends, with their hectic, tense, lives, use our weekend retreats for inspiration.

At our house, friends arrive throughout the weekend. Friday nights, everyone is on their own. They come in groups of twos and threes by car, by the Hampton Jitney, or the Long Island Railroad. Guests drive out from the city at ten or eleven at night, arriving as late as two o'clock in the morning. An open-door policy is a house custom, since by this time, Nancy and I have retired. A simple note of greeting tells them which bedroom is theirs for the weekend. Our open-door policy includes the refrigerator, and many a guest has raided the icebox for his or her own late-night inventions.

In order to be able to enjoy having so many guests, we had to develop a more relaxed style of entertaining. Our traditional Southern upbringing had certain rules about how to be a good host, but early in our lives, we had to learn how to alter these customs to allow us to enjoy this fellowship of friends in our home.

SOUTHERN BRUNCH MENU

Frittata Andre
Country Ham Steak with Red-Eye Gravy
Cheese Puddin'
Sautéed Kale
Dill Corn Bread

25

Breakfast Breads

I rise early on Saturdays to enjoy the amazing early morning light outside our windows. The short drive I take to the village of East Hampton and the visit I make to our village's gourmet emporium, the Barefoot Contessa, is a wonderful experience filled with sights, aromas, and sounds. Early risers join me in this sojourn. We are culinary voyeurs. This little market is an early meeting place for people from all over the Hamptons who are preparing for their weekend houseful.

When I was a child in my village in Alabama, fettucini, quiche, sushi, and guacamole were unheard of. Today, many Americans have become connoisseurs of international fare. Over the last decade, all over America, specialty food markets have taken root. They have sprung up in both our large urban centers and small villages. These big and small businesses make it wonderfully convenient to offer their unique treats to your friends and guests. On our country weekends, it seems impractical or unfeasible to spend hours baking breads when you can easily select and buy a range of fresh loaves from your local specialty market.

A CORNUCOPIA OF BUTTERS

Serves 8–10

Ingredients:
For each fruit butter:
½ cup whipped sweet butter, room temperature
¼ cup jam, either strawberry, apricot, blueberry, blackberry or a few of your favorites.

1. With fork, in bowl, mix ½ cup butter with a flavor of jam, combining well.
2. Press each combination into a decorative serving piece. The different flavors and colorations add a festive touch to breads and muffins.

26

Frittata Andre

Our group of friends all look forward to our weekends when Andre Smith is our guest. When Andre comes, we all step back and let the master chef take command of the kitchen. Consultation occurs around morning coffee, tea, and breads. Andre selects a sous-chef, his lieutenant in the kitchen. Menus are planned and shopping lists are made. Brunch in our household is in the early afternoon, after visits to the market, a short viewing of the beach, or springtime sojourns to the nursery. At about two o'clock, after a flurry of activity in the kitchen, Andre and I have prepared a festive dish for everyone to enjoy.

GOLDEN PEPPER FRITTATA

Serves 4–6

Ingredients:

2 chorizo or hot Italian sausages, in ¼" slices
2 tablespoons olive oil
1 large potato, peeled and thinly sliced
1 sweet red pepper, cleaned and coarsely chopped
1 green pepper, cleaned and chopped
1 onion, coarsely chopped
salt and pepper to taste
several sprigs fresh parsley, finely chopped
¼ cup half-and-half or milk
1 pinch of ground caraway seeds
a pinch of freshly ground nutmeg
8 eggs

1. Preheat over to 425°.
2. In black iron skillet sauté chorizo sausage in olive oil until almost done, approximately 4–5 minutes. Hot sausage may need more time.
3. Add potato slices and sauté 2–3 minutes until almost tender.
4. Add peppers and onion, salt and pepper to taste, and sauté until onions are transparent, about 5 minutes.
5. Add parsley. Stir and set aside.
6. In a large bowl, whisk together eggs, half-and-half, caraway, and nutmeg until lightly beaten.
7. Add egg mixture to pan, cover, and cook over low heat for 5 minutes until bottom of frittata is set.
8. Loosen from pan with spatula onto large plate, soft side up.
9. Turn pan over on frittata and flip over so frittata is now soft-side down in the pan.
Continue cooking 3–5 minutes until frittata reaches consistency you desire. If a soft moist frittata is desired, turn out on a warm platter and serve.
10. If a firm frittata is preferred, put in oven and cook an additional 3–5 minutes until frittata is cooked through and puffs up like a shallow soufflé. Turn out on a warm platter and serve.

Frittata is turned onto my golden-banded terra-cotta service plates and placed on golden doily place mats. Napkins of overscaled terry towels are ringed in a golden cuff of acorns. Parsley or seasonal greens are on the table to be pinched off as garnish if desired.

Cheese Puddin'

Grits are as old as America itself. This much-loved Southern grain is just beginning to be found in markets around America. In the 1600s, the Indians in Jamestown offered soft maize, seasoned with salt and cooked bird or meat drippings, to the early settlers. The Indians called it rockahominie, and our forefathers shortened the name to hominy. Before long, they were milling hominy into finer grains and grits came into being. A popular regional food, it is traditionally served as a morning hot cereal. New York City, with its great contingent of Southern folk, is one of the largest grits consumers outside of the South. Quaker Oats, the country's biggest supplier of grits, now sells them in every state of the union.

DOWN-HOME SOUTHERN GRITS

Serves 4–6

Ingredients:
water
1 cup grits
1 teaspoon salt

1. Boil 4 cups of water in medium-sized saucepan.
2. Stir in grits slowly. Add salt.
3. Cook 15 to 20 minutes, stirring occasionally until thick.

Whether at home or in the local diner, most Southern breakfasts are accompanied by this hot cereal. These 2 classic garnishes are basic Southern fare.

RICH AND SHARP

Fold in butter to taste and crack whole peppercorns over the cereal for a rich and sharp version.

SWEET AND SAVORY

Fold in brown or white sugar and cream to taste. This classic preparation is similar to hot oatmeal but with its own distinctive taste.

From these simple beginnings, the grain is being used in new and inventive ways. Cheese Grits Puddin', a twist of Andre's, is one of my favorites.

CHEESE PUDDIN'

Serves 4–6

Ingredients:
1 cup grits, uncooked
4 cups water
1 tablespoon salt
1 stick butter
1 egg, beaten
1 8-ounce pkg. Boursin cheese
½ pound sharp cheddar cheese
2 tablespoons Worcestershire sauce
dash of Tabasco
2 tablespoons chopped jalapeño peppers
paprika

1. Preheat over to 350°.
2. Put grits, water, and water in large pot.
3. Bring to a boil, then reduce flame and cook 5–8 minutes, stirring often for smooth consistency.
4. Add remaining ingredients except paprika. Stir until cheeses melt.
5. Select a terra-cotta or other special casserole to use as a service dish and grease with butter. Pour mixture into dish.
6. Sprinkle with paprika and bake for 30 minutes.

Another variation is Spinach Cheese Puddin'.

Southern Greens

Stewed and sautéed country greens are traditional Southern fare. Many of our Southern delicacies can be traced to African territories and this food is at the heart of "soul" cooking. As Southern culture evolved, a family of greens, from turnip greens to collard greens to kale, could be found on all tables, from the most modest cabins to the grandest plantation dining rooms. Large bowls of greens in their liquor, garnished with sweet corn bread, taste as delicious today as they do in treasured memories. Andre, with his Caribbean heritage, has brought his own variations to this beloved soul food.

RAYMOND'S COLLARD GREENS

Serves 6–8

Ingredients:

6 thick slices bacon, ⅛" each
1 tablespoon freshly cracked pepper
1 pound of fresh collard greens in season washed, with tough center stem removed or 2 10-ounce packages frozen collard greens, thawed or 2 14-oz. cans collard greens
water to cover
½ teaspoon salt
2 tablespoons sugar.

1. In a medium-sized saucepan sauté bacon over high heat until juices are extracted and bacon is crisp.
2. Break bacon into bits and garnish with black pepper.
3. Add fresh or thawed greens to pan with bacon and pepper. Cover with water.
4. Add salt and sugar, cover pan, and let simmer a minimum of 1 hour, adding water as necessary to create a rich liquor.
5. Serve hot with Southern corn bread.

"Down-home style" is to serve greens with corn bread. The corn bread is broken and crumbled into the green liquor and creates a pudding-like dish. A real Southern treat. If in your farmer's market there are fresh collard greens in season, this same recipe can be used with them and turnip. The turnip should be peeled and cut in very coarse sections approximately ½"–¾" in size. "Down-home style" greens should be simmered for several hours until greens and turnips are tender and breaking apart.

ANDRE'S KALE AND BACON

Serves 6

Ingredients:

2 large bunches of kale (collard, turnip, or mustard greens can be substituted)
4 thick slices bacon
3 cloves garlic, peeled and crushed
½ cup water
salt and pepper to taste

1. Wash greens and remove tough center stem. Chop coarsely.
2. Sauté bacon in large pot to release juices and to crisp.
3. Brown 2 cloves garlic in bacon fat, continuing to stir.
4. Add greens and stir until wilted, approximately 3 minutes.
5. Add water, salt, and pepper. Cover and simmer at low heat until tender, approximately 15 minutes.
6. Add remaining garlic and stir at high heat to evaporate remaining liquid.
7. Serve hot.

Alabama Red-Eye

Certain familiar foods from our Southern heritage are perfect country weekend fare. Country ham, a down-home favorite, was a new taste for most of our friends from around America. For brunch, country ham served with cheese grits, kale, and frittata adds an exotic touch to soul food by Chef Andre.

Our country buffet table is laden with country ham floating in a bed of red-eye gravy, garnished with sautéed onions and kale, and displayed on a nineteenth-century English export platter with traditional Oriental motifs. Golden doilies cover hot pads to protect the buffet table from casseroles recently removed from the oven and earthenware bowls of kale. Golden rabbits among buffet plates of green majolica and gold-gilded flatware finish the setting.

DILLED CORN BREAD

Serves 8

Ingredients:
1 8½ oz. package of Jiffy corn muffin mix
1 egg
⅓ cup milk
¼ cup fresh dill, finely chopped, or 1 tablespoon dried dill

1. Preheat oven to 400°.
2. Grease muffin or bread pan.
3. Fold ingredients together. Leave batter slightly lumpy.
4. Pour batter in greased muffin or bread pan and bake 15 to 20 minutes until golden brown.

COUNTRY HAM STEAK WITH RED-EYE GRAVY

Serves 4–6

Ingredients:
1 large ham steak,
cut into ¾"-thick piece, fully cooked
4 tablespoons butter
2 large white onions,
peeled and coarsely chopped
½ cup brewed coffee
pinch of sugar
salt and pepper to taste

1. Heat oven to 250°.
2. In iron skillet, sauté ham steak in 2 tablespoons butter until lightly brown on both sides.
3. Remove to ovenproof platter and reserve in warm oven.
4. To make gravy, sauté onions in pan juices until transparent and caramelized.
5. Add coffee and stir.
6. Add sugar, salt, and pepper.
7. Bring sauce to boil. Add remaining butter, moving pan rapidly and continuously until sauce is thickened.
8. Pour gravy over the ham steak and serve.

For special lunches, our farm table beside the pool is dressed with branches of leaves from the woods. Golden doilies are used as place mats under terra-cotta plates. Terry towels for napkins rest under a mix of utensils held together by a golden napkin ring. Silver samovars and urns are full of gin and tonics ready for our first toast.

Sweet and Tart

aturday night, whether the group is large or small, is the time for our most lavish meal. We've had time to prepare our menus, shop for ingredients, and make ready. Andre begins his artistry with his appointed lieutenant. As the sun is setting, part of the group is relaxing around the pool or taking a short nap. Magical things begin to occur. Aromas and laughter fill the house. Drinks are served. Andre, a very particular chef, gives commands like a captain on the deck of his ship. Peppers are sliced, vegetables chopped, salad greens and fruits are washed, and salmon is grilled.

HONEY DILL

Serves 6–8

Ingredients:
½ cup hon
12 dill pick

1. Pour hon
vase.
2. Insert pickle spears into honey and arrange like a bouquet of flowers.

GULF COAST MENU

Orange and Onion Salad
Jalapeño Succotash
Grilled Salmon with Cilantro Pesto
Melon and Raspberries in Cranberry
Dream Sauce

ORANGE AND ONION SALAD

Serves 6–8

Ingredients:
6–8 large navel oranges
1 large red onion
2 tablespoons cracked whole pepper

1. Peel onion and cut into ¼″ rings.
2. Peel oranges and cut into ¼″ slices as shown.
3. Layer onions on bottom of platter so that onion slices touch.
4. Layer oranges on top of onions so that slices touch each other.
5. Repeat layering to create thin layers of orange and onion so the flavors mingle.
6. Sprinkle profusely with cracked pepper.
7. Serve with Cranberry Dream Sauce on page 44.

Salad is served in a country colander of green-ware. Terry towels are used throughout the buffet as napkins as well as pads to protect the table from heat and moisture.

Jalapeño Succotash

PEPPER BASKET

One per guest

Succotash is served in red pepper baskets prepared while ingredients are simmering. Slice off the head of 1 sweet red pepper for each guest. Remove seeds and clean shell. Trim base as shown so pepper stands. Set aside.

One of the recipes I asked Andre for is his Jalapeño Succotash. The combination of flavors is tart and mellow and the visual impact creates a festive mood.

JALAPEÑO SUCCOTASH IN PEPPER BASKETS

Serves 6–8
Ingredients:
5 slices bacon, julienned after 1 hour in the freezer
1 cup cherry tomatoes for garnish
1 sweet yellow pepper
1 sweet red pepper
2–3 jalapeño peppers
10 ears fresh corn in season, or 2 10-ounce packages, frozen
1½ cups frozen baby lima beans, thawed, or fresh in summer
pinch of sugar
pinch of salt
½ cup water
freshly ground pepper

1. Sauté bacon in large pan until crisp. Remove from pan. Set aside.
2. Briefly sauté cherry tomatoes in bacon drippings to brown slightly. Remove from pan and set aside.
3. Sauté sweet and jalapeño peppers in remaining bacon drippings.
4. Add water. Cover and steam at low heat for 12–20 minutes.
5. Mix in freshly ground pepper, fill each pepper with the mixture, and garnish with sautéed cherry tomatoes.

For a festive presentation of this colorful mix, my collection of majolica was the ideal background. When presenting any food, think of its color and how it will look on serving dishes. The rich play of yellows, reds, and greens has more impact when surrounded by these rich, green vessels, accented with antique horn spoons from the Portobello Road market in London.

Salmon Pesto

almon is sweet in flavor and has a beautiful soft pink coloring. This large fillet of salmon has been grilled and set in a nest of fresh greens on a large wooden cutting board. Greens are endive, red leaf, Boston, and romaine lettuce. The salmon has been garnished with pesto sauce, scattered sweet red peppers, and black pepper, cracked with mortar and pestle for texture. A part of all of our evening meals is the glow of candlelight. In recent years, since the opening of Russia, marvelous Russian candlesticks are appearing in the antique fairs. Here these silver over brass treasures are used in contrast to the utilitarian cutting board serving piece.

GRILLED SALMON WITH CILANTRO PESTO

Serves 6–8
Ingredients:
1 large salmon fillet or 1 small salmon steak per person, approximately 8 ounces each.
½ lime
olive oil for basting
pinch of salt and pepper
assorted fresh greens: endive, red leaf, Boston, or romaine lettuce

1. Rinse salmon in cold water.
2. Squeeze juice of ½ lime over salmon.
3. Brush with olive oil.
4. Sprinkle with salt and pepper.
5. Grill over low coals until done. Timing depends on size and thickness of salmon. When done, center of salmon should be cooked and firm, but just barely so.

CILANTRO PESTO SAUCE

Serves 6–8

Ingredients:
2 cups of cilantro, washed and trimmed
½ medium white onion
½ jalapeño pepper
½ cup lime juice
½–¾ cup olive oil

1. Puree all ingredients except olive oil in blender or food processor.
2. Add olive oil in a slow stream until sauce reaches your favorite consistency.
3. Serve at room temperature with grilled salmon and greens.

A Golden Nest

pring and summer are times when the freshest fruits are readily available. Nothing is faster to prepare than nature's bounty presented in its own nest. The setting has been framed first by a 12-inch golden charger plate. Then I placed a green majolica leaf plate on top to accent the golden tones of the ripe melon or papaya. Rich ruby raspberries have been mounded in the cavity of the melon, and a golden shell is used as a sugar cellar for garnish.

MELON AND RASPBERRIES, IN SAUCE

Serves 4–6
Ingredients:
½ ripe melon (whatever is in season)
2 cups raspberries
sugar to taste

1. Cut melon in half lengthwise. Discard seeds.
2. Scoop out flesh with a small spoon.
3. Cascade raspberries and melon flesh in and around the melon shell.

CRANBERRY DREAM SAUCE

Ingredients:
15-ounce can whole-berry cranberry sauce
½ cup sour cream
½ cup mayonnaise
2 tablespoons cracked whole pepper (or to taste)

1. Mix all ingredients together. If a creamier sauce is desired, more sour cream and mayonnaise can be added.
2. Crack whole pepper with a mortar and pestle. I like the tangy flavor abundant pepper adds to this sweet sauce. Limit the amount of pepper to your palate.
3. Chill briefly, then serve.

This makes enough sauce for 12 plentiful servings. It can be stored in the refrigerator for up to two weeks.

LIGHT CRANBERRY DREAM SAUCE

Ingredients:
15-ounce can of whole cranberry sauce
1 cup vanilla yogurt
¼ cup cracked pepper

1. Follow instructions for Cranberry Dream Sauce, above.

FESTIVE TABLES

For Summer Treats

Recipes,
Menus, and Tablesettings
for Every Occasion

For Nancy and me, summer begins with the Memorial Day weekend. The Hamptons come alive with people. The streets are full of activity. The city fathers are preparing for the Memorial Day and Fourth of July parades. People are opening their houses, making ready for the warm sun of summer.

The Hamptons dress up in great costumes for these events. Red, white, and blue fill the streets at both Memorial Day and Fourth of July, putting everyone in a festive mood. In the farmers' markets the earliest summer bounty is beginning to appear. The Hamptons possess vast fields of strawberries offering sweet aromatic treats ready for picking. Throughout the season, fields of salad greens, tomatoes, corn, and fresh flowers are harvested daily and appear on farm stands in all the villages.

The Hamptons are located on a narrow slip of land surrounded by the Atlantic

This is the year of the sun. Everywhere — in antique shops, magazines, on table settings, and in decorative details — the golden sun is rising. For Memorial Day and Fourth of July, homes as well as shops display their patriotism.

SUMMER'S EVE MENU

Lots of strawberries
Lots of shrimp
Fruit Coolers

What more do you need?

Ocean and Long Island Sound. It has been a haven for our fishing industry for centuries. In the afternoon, expeditions to the Amagansett farmers' market, Round Swamp Farms, and Stewart's Fish Market reward us with the freshest harvest of the sea.

In the dog days of summer, white sangria, lemonade and lemon ice are always welcome.

WHITE SANGRIA

Serves 24

Ingredients:
1 dozen navel oranges, washed, cut into wedges (do not peel)
6 limes, washed, cut into wedges, remove seeds
½ ripe honeydew melon, flesh seeded and cut into bite-sized wedges
3 cups seedless white grapes, washed, halved
2 cups sugar
2 cups Triple Sec
3 bottles chardonnay wine (750 ML)
3 bottles white zinfandel wine (750 ML)
cracked ice

1. In a large punch bowl, squeeze juice from orange and lime wedges and put fruit into bowl after squeezing.
2. Add melon and grapes. Cover with sugar. Stir to dissolve.
3. Add remaining ingredients. Mix well, add lots of cracked ice, and serve.

WHITE LEMONADE

Individual serving
Ingredients:
3–4 tablespoons sugar
½ cup water
1½ tablespoons freshly squeezed lemon juice
½ cup club soda
1 cup white grape juice
mint leaf

1. Boil sugar and water for 1–2 minutes, stirring to mix. Set aside and chill.
2. Add lemon juice, club soda, and white grape juice. Serve over ice in large tumbler.
3. Garnish with mint leaf or fruit, if desired.

LEMON ICE

Serves 4–6

Ingredients:
2 cups sugar
1 tablespoon lemon peel, grated
¾ cup lemon juice
½ cup white grape juice

1. Boil 3 cups of water and add sugar to dissolve.
2. Cool, then add all other ingredients.
3. Pour into 3 or 4 ice cube trays and freeze.
4. Serve with lemonade, orange, cranberry or grape juice.

Farm Fresh Strawberries

The start of summer for us is always defined by the aroma of fresh strawberries. Though high-speed distribution of fruits from around the world make strawberries available year-round, there is something special about vine-ripened strawberries. Nothing could be more spectacular than vessels full of this simple treat.

FARM FRESH STRAWBERRIES

Serves 8–10

4 pint baskets strawberries
½ cup sugar

1. Wash strawberries in cold water. Do not remove stems.
2. Layer over cracked ice in large over-scaled vessels or baskets.

STRAWBERRY DIPS

Serve with stems attached so guests can dip into
granulated or confectioners' sugar,
sweet cream,
lemon yogurt,
chocolate syrup,
or multicolored sprinkles for the kids.

CREAM TOPPING

Serves 6–8
Ingredients:
2½ cups half-and-half
½ cup quick grits
3 tablespoons honey
¼ teaspoon salt
1 teaspoon vanilla or almond extract
slivered almonds for garnish

1. In a saucepan, bring half-and-half, grits, honey, and salt to a boil.
2. Stir 5–8 minutes while boiling to obtain a smooth consistency.
3. Lower heat and cook until thickened, approximately 5 minutes. Stir often.
4. Fold in vanilla or almond extract.
5. Sprinkle with slivered almonds.
6. Serve warm over sliced peaches, strawberries, raspberries, or other fruit of the season.

Summer Coolers

On late afternoon, after returning from the beach, antique fairs, or sojourns to the farmers' markets, a quick dip in the pool, followed by a fruit cooler, sets the tone for an evening's fantasy.

Our friend Mario Commacho is great at blending a combination of elixirs to put us all in a great mood. These drinks are fun to experiment with once you learn the basic mix. Fresh fruits can be combined with various ways to create different taste treats.

A creative choice of glassware makes any drink more special. I use elegant champagne flutes for many occasions, both casual and formal. Garnish with lime, lemon, or other fruit wedges.

STRAWBERRY COOLER

Serves 4–6

Ingredients:
6–8 strawberries, depending on size
cracked ice to fill blender
½ (6 ounce) can strawberry daiquiri mix
rum to taste

1. Wash and stem strawberries.
2. Put into blender.
3. Cover with cracked ice.
4. Add daiquiri mix and rum to taste.
5. Blend ingredients until smooth. Add additional ice as needed. Blend to consistency that a straw will stand in. If necessary, remove a portion of the liquid to a pitcher and add more ice to the blender to create the desired thickness.

BANANA COOLER

Serves 4–6
Ingredients:
1–2 ripe bananas
cracked ice
½ small can concentrated apple juice
1 jigger banana liqueur or to taste
rum to taste

1. Peel bananas. Put in blender.
2. Cover with cracked ice.
3. Add apple juice.
4. Add banana liqueur.
5. Add rum to taste.
6. Blend to smooth consistency so a straw will stand up in glass. Add ice as needed to obtain desired consistency.

MARIO'S SURPRISE

Serves approximately 20

Ingredients:
2 ripe peaches
1 ripe banana
2, 2-inch slices of cantaloupe
½ cup blueberries
½ cup strawberries
peach brandy to taste
rum to taste
1 6-ounce can strawberry daiquiri mix

1. Wash and prepare all fruit.
2. Put fruit, brandy, rum and daiquiri mix in blender. Blend until smooth.
3. Remove ½ of the mixture and put into pitcher.
4. Add ice to blender to cover the rest, and continue to blend until the mixture is of the desired consistency. Serve garnished with ½ strawberry.
5. Process reserved mixture with ice for "the other half."

When preparing coolers for larger groups, the fruit and liqueur mixture can be made in advance. Refrigerate and mix with ice when served.

Sea Fresh Shrimp

SHRIMP WITH 7 SAUCES

Serves 8

Ingredients:
water to cover
1 (3-ounce) package Crab Boil (a combination of spices available in food and seafood markets)
1–2 tablespoons of olive oil depending on amount of water
3 pounds of medium shrimp in the shell (allow 8–10 per person)
lime wedges
parsley

1. Bring water to hard boil. Add Crab Boil and olive oil.
2. Add shrimp.
3. Reduce heat and cook 2 minutes. Shrimp will turn a beautiful pink color. Do not overcook.
4. Turn into colander to drain.
5. Rinse under cold water to stop cooking process.
6. Put in refrigerator to cool until ready for serving.
7. Serve over cracked ice in large vessel or basket.
8. Garnish with lime wedges and parsley.

QUICK REMOULADE SAUCE
(Sauce 1)
1 cup mayonnaise
3 tablespoons Dijon mustard
2 tablespoons lemon juice
1 teaspoon white wine vinegar
4 tablespoons drained capers
3 tablespoons chopped parsley
1 tablespoon fresh tarragon or ½ tablespoon dried

1. In a blender combine mayonnaise, mustards, lemon juice, and white wine vinegar and process for 30 seconds.
2. Add remaining ingredients and process until smooth.
3. Chill before serving.

COCKTAIL SAUCE
(Sauce 2)
cup favorite bottled cocktail sauce or ketchup
juice of ½ lemon
horseradish to taste

1. Mix all ingredients. Add horseradish to taste for a more spicy, tangy sauce.
2. Chill before serving.

TARTAR SAUCE
(Sauce 3)
1 cup your preferred brand of tartar sauce

CURRIED MAYONNAISE
(Sauce 4)
1 cup mayonnaise
2 tablespoons curry powder, or to taste

1. Mix all ingredients.
2. Chill before serving.

CHUTNEY
(Sauce 5)
1 cup your favorite chutney sauce
(I prefer Earl Grey mango chutney.)

1. Serve at room temperature

DILL AND MELTED BUTTER
(Sauce 6)
2 sticks salted butter, melted
¼ cup fresh dill, finely chopped

1. Combine ingredients. Do not chill.
2. Serve at room temperature.

HONEY MUSTARD
(Sauce 7)
½ cup Dijon mustard
2 tablespoons honey
½ teaspoon mustard seeds

1. Combine all ingredients.
2. Serve at room temperature.

Summer Treats

A n easy lunch that's light and always enjoyed is a simple salad of fruit. Our markets are full of berries and melons. The preparation is a breeze, but the dish invites endless combinations. Served with Cranberry Dream Sauce (page 44), fresh fruit salad is the essence of summer.

CORNUCOPIA OF FRUIT

Serves 8–10

Ingredients:
1 quarter-section of watermelon, wedged
3 navel oranges, peeled, separate sections
3 nectarines, seeded and sliced
½ cantaloupe, peeled, seeded, and cut into chunks
½ honeydew melon, peeled, seeded, and cut into chunks
purple grapes taken off the stem
1 pint strawberries, leaves and stems removed
½ pint raspberries

1. Wash all fruit except melon.
2. Cut up as shown and layer in order of ingredients in large bowl.

As an hors d'oeuvre in the afternoon, melon and oranges sliced and skewered are simply elegant refreshments when served with lemon yogurt and topped with ground nutmeg.

A Gathering of Mushrooms

Sheaves of varied pastas are available for new adventures in dining. From left to right:
1. Beet Onion in a deep, rich rose coloration;
2. Rafaela's Herb with its greenish tint;
3. Chili Cilantro colored burnished orange;
4. Red Bell Pepper in natural oatmeal tones;
4. Ginger Garlic Linguine is a classic pasta color;
6. Saffron Linguine has a spicy, golden orange glow.

Our markets are full of mushrooms. Shiitake, porcini, morels, chanterelles offer a wide range of flavors and textures easy to serve as a side dish or as a main course for vegetarians. Combined with pasta, they provide a robust, full-bodied meal. There seems to be no limit to the sizes, shapes, and colors of pastas available today. The combinations you can experiment with are endless.

SHIITAKE, PORCINI, AND CREMINI OVER BEET ONION PASTA

Serves 6–8

Ingredients:
2 large Spanish (purple) onions, peeled and coarsely chopped
½ cup olive oil
2 cups large porcini mushrooms brushed clean of dirt or sand, caps sliced in eighths
3 cups small shiitake mushrooms brushed clean of dirt or sand, whole
2 cups cremini brushed clean of dirt or sand, cut in half lengthwise
1 tablespoon freshly cracked black pepper
2 tablespoons flour
2 cups chicken broth, more if needed to create the consistency of a thick sauce
a bunch of Italian or curly leaf parsley, washed, dried, and coarsely chopped

1. In a large pan sauté onions in the olive oil until they begin to soften.
2. Add porcini mushrooms, and sauté over high heat.
3. Add shiitakes and cremini and stir-fry. Lower heat and cook until mushrooms give up juices, 3–5 minutes.
4. Add pepper and flour to mixture and fold in until flour disappears.
5. Add chicken broth slowly. Stir and cook until sauce thickens, approximately 1 minute.
6. Serve over pasta and garnish profusely with parsley.

Toss pasta with a tablespoon of olive oil to ensure pasta does not stick, then surround it with the mushroom sauce. Garnish liberally with chopped parsley as shown.

Coconut Cloud

Nancy is an artist at baking. In our circle of friends, she's always chosen to prepare their favorite birthday cake, whether it's rich chocolate cake or this Coconut Cloud. For summer weekends, this family favorite is on hand for weekend guests, with coffee in the morning or as the finale to a Saturday night's festivities.

POPPY SEED CAKE

Serves 8–10

Ingredients:
½ cup poppy seeds
1 cup milk
¾ cup butter (softened)
½ cup sugar
2 egg yolks
2 cups flour
2 teaspoons baking powder
2 egg whites

1. Soak poppy seeds in milk overnight.
2. Preheat oven to 350°.
3. Cream butter and sugar.
4. Beat in egg yolks.
5. Add milk and poppy seeds.
6. Mix in flour and baking powder.
7. Beat in egg whites.
8. Pour mixture into 2 buttered, floured 8 ½" cake pans.
9. Bake at 350° for 40 minutes. Remove from oven and cool.
10. Frost with Coconut Cloud Frosting.

COCONUT CLOUD FROSTING

Ingredients:
¼ cup water
1 large egg white
¼ cup sugar
¼ teaspoon cream of tartar
1 teaspoon vanilla extract
½ teaspoon almond extract
1½–2 bags packaged coconut, shredded

1. Place all ingredients except coconut in the top of a double boiler.
2. Fill bottom of double boiler with 2 inches of boiling water.
3. Beat ingredients with electric beater until frosting stands in soft, stiff peaks. Be sure water continues to boil.
4. Remove from heat and continue beating until frosting stands in very stiff peaks.
5. Spread over cold cake.
6. Sprinkle coconut over frosting.

For a festive bit of fun on my birthday, Nancy dressed our geese decoys in necklaces of multicolored balloons. The same color theme was carried through the house in baskets of gifts wrapped in tissue paper and festive ribbons. The deck was surrounded with crockery filled with country roses.

Fourth of July

Fourth of July is a festive holiday all across America. After fireworks in Manhattan's or East Hampton's harbors have set the mood for patriotic revelry, a party with classic American food, simple, hearty and well loved was what we wanted. This year, a set of red, white, and blue napkins with fields of stars set the patriotic Americana theme.

Our buffet table has been set with squares of napkins in red, white, and blue in a checkerboard pattern. The centerpiece of country roses and blue hydrangea repeats the color theme.

STARS AND STRIPES MENU

Champagne or Mimosas
Americana Salad
Raymond's Basic Chili or
Nancy's Too-Hot-to-Trot Chili
Pan-sauteed Hot Dogs
Garlic Toasted Buns
Grilled Vegetables
A Parade of Desserts

Sparklers

In restaurants and markets this year, Ty Nant, a new springwater from Wales, appeared in an intense cobalt blue bottle. When I and many of my friends first saw these bottles in restaurants we asked to take them home. They look beautiful on our buffet. For presentation, I started with a basket and covered the inside with a plastic garbage bag, concealed in turn with a red-starred napkin. Cubed ice rendered the basket an instant ice bucket.

A festive gathering doesn't always demand alcoholic drinks, and dieters have to avoid them as well. With this mind, we have developed a range of refreshing "splashes" that are brightly colored, healthy and delicious. All of them look good garnished with a piece of fruit or a sprig of mint.

SPLISH/SPLASH

Serves 1

1 large glass sparkling water
splash of orange, or cranberry, or purple grape juice.

1. Combine all ingredients and serve over ice.

ORANGEBERRY SPLISH/SPLASH

Serves 1

Ingredients:
½ cup sparkling water
1 cup orange or grapefruit juice
¼ cup cranberry juice

1. Combine all ingredients. Serve over cracked ice.

APRICOT SPLISH/SPLASH

Serves 1

Ingredients:
½ cup apricot nectar
1 cup white grape juice
½ cup sparkling water

1. Combine all ingredients and serve over ice.

PINEAPPLE SPLISH/SPLASH

Serves 1

Ingredients:
1 cup pineapple juice
¼ cup pina colada mix
½ cup ginger ale

1. Combine all ingredients and serve over ice.
2. Serve with strawberries.

CHAMPAGNE SPLISH/SPLASH

In all the refreshers above, champagne can be used instead of tonic, water or ginger ale for a variation with alcohol.

68

Vegetarian Grill

Peppers of all colors—red, orange, yellow, and green—have become new, festive staples of my cooking. At certain times of the year they are expensive but well worth it. Their sweet flavor and gorgeous color are great additions to many menus. On summer weekends, they are a breeze to grill. When charred and burned over a high flame, they take on a sweet and sharp flavor. Other vegetables—zucchini, eggplant, onions, and potatoes, both Idaho and sweet—are also wonderful prepared this way, alone or over your favorite pasta garnished with blanched French green beans.

GRILLED VEGETABLES

Serves 6–8

Ingredients:
2 red peppers
2 yellow peppers
2 orange peppers
1 onion
¼ cup olive oil
1 zucchini
1 Idaho potato
1 sweet potato
2 baby eggplants

1. Wash and clean all vegetables.
2. Slice peppers and onion into sections. Brush with oil.
3. Slice zucchini, potatoes, and eggplants on the diagonal. Brush with oil.
4. Thread the vegetable slices on skewers to prevent their burning and falling through the grill.
5. Grill over a bed of charcoal, turning frequently until lightly charred.
6. Serve hot or at room temperature.

For Nancy and me, chili con carne is one of the most American of foods. For small family dinners or large potluck suppers, chili goes from simple get-togethers to grand party gatherings. You can serve it alone, with different toppings, like sour cream and chives, onions, or grated cheddar cheese, or over hot dogs, burgers, or steak. The traditional presentation of hot dogs in a bun with chili topping is as American as apple pie.

RAYMOND'S BASIC CHILI

Serves 6–8

Ingredients:
2 large green peppers, seeded and sliced
2 large yellow onions, peeled and diced
¼ cup olive oil
1¼ pounds ground beef
1 can (16 ounces) kidney beans
1 bottle (12 ounces) of chili sauce

1. Brown peppers and onions in oil.
2. Add ground beef and brown.
3. Add beans and sauce and simmer 20 minutes.
4. Serve over hot dogs, burgers, or steak.

NANCY'S TOO-HOT-TO-TROT CHILI

Serves 6–8

Ingredients:
½ stick salted butter
1 large green pepper, seeded and sliced
2 large yellow onions, peeled and coarsely diced
2 pounds ground beef
1 package frozen corn kernels, thawed
2 (16 ounce) cans red kidney beans
1 package of Two Alarm Chili spices

1. Melt butter in large pan. Brown peppers and onions until soft.
2. Add ground beef and brown.
3. Add beans, corn, and chili spices and simmer 20 minutes.

PAN-SAUTÉED HOT DOGS

Serves 6–8

Ingredients:
½ Spanish (purple) onion, peeled and coarsely chopped
12–16 hot dogs, 2 per person
¼ cup olive oil

1. In a large iron skillet, sauté onions and hot dogs in oil until brown. I like the dogs slightly burned for a charred flavor. (Onions and dogs can be grilled over charcoal if available.)
2. Serve in garlic toasted buns.

GARLIC TOASTED BUNS

Serves 6–8

Ingredients:
1 stick salted butter
3 cloves of garlic, peeled and finely chopped
1 tablespoon dried oregano
hot dog buns, 2 per person

1. Melt butter in small saucepan. Do not brown.
2. Add garlic and oregano.
3. Remove from heat and brush over hot dog buns.
4. Toast under high flame in broiler until golden brown.

I Cannot Tell a Lie

The story has George Washington issuing this phrase and cherry pie into American folklore. My mother's cherry pie on George Washington's birthday is a fond childhood memory. It was one of the first recipes I asked for after Nancy and I married so that it could become a part of our table. We have shortened the procedure by using packaged piecrust. Nancy has found that Flako and Jiffy are both great and easy to use.

GEORGE WASHINGTON'S TREAT

Serves 6–8
Ingredients:

CRUST

Prepare Flako or Jiffy crust as directed.

CHERRY FILLING

Ingredients:
3 cups fresh or canned dark Bing cherries, stemmed and pitted if fresh
1 cup granulated sugar
1½ tablespoons flour
1 teaspoon vanilla
1 teaspoon almond extract
2 tablespoons sweet butter

1. Preheat oven to 350°.
2. Roll out entire package of piecrust into a circle and line an 8" pie pan allowing crust to drape over the edges.
3. Drain cherries if canned, saving approximately ½ the liquor.
4. Mix liquor, sugar, flour, and vanilla and almond extracts in a bowl. (If using fresh cherries, the natural juices will flow when cooked and are sufficient.)
5. Pour mixture into piecrust.
6. Dot with butter.
7. Fold edges of crust as shown in photograph to create unique cover with open center.
8. Bake 40–50 minutes or until crust is lightly brown.

For presentation, I have encircled pie with country crockery, blue and white stars, and country baskets.

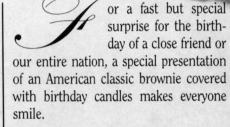

Happy Birthday America

For a fast but special surprise for the birthday of a close friend or our entire nation, a special presentation of an American classic brownie covered with birthday candles makes everyone smile.

HAPPY BIRTHDAY BROWNIES

Serves 6–8

Ingredients:
3 ounces unsweetened chocolate
6 tablespoons sweet butter
1½ cups granulated sugar
3 large eggs, beaten
1 tablespoon ground cinnamon
1 tablespoon almond extract
¾ cup flour
1½ cups chopped pecans
1½ teaspoons vanilla
1 12 ounce package of chocolate chips

1. Preheat oven to 350°.
2. Melt chocolate and butter in double boiler. Stir constantly to a smooth consistency. Remove from heat.
3. Fold in sugar, eggs, cinnamon, almond extract, flour, pecans, and chocolate chips.

4. Butter a 9″-square pan. Pour in mixture.
5. Bake in oven approximately 40 minutes or until top is crusty. Don't overcook. Brownies are better when moist and chewy.
6. Remove pan from oven and let cool. Cut brownies into squares. Insert 4–5 candles in each and sing "Happy Birthday" to America.

BROWNIE SANDWICH

For a special treat that is always loved by young guests, cut 1 brownie square in half and cover 1 side with chunky peanut butter or raspberry jam, like a sandwich. Close and serve.

RED, WHITE AND BERRY FILLING

Ingredients:
3 tablespoons flour
1 cup granulated sugar
2 cups fresh blueberries, washed
1 tablespoon lemon juice
1 teaspoon vanilla extract
1 teaspoon almond extract
1 package Jiffy or Flako piecrust, prepared as directed
2 cups fresh strawberries, washed, stems removed, halved
1 tablespoon sweet butter

1. Preheat oven to 350°.
2. Combine flour and sugar in a large bowl.
3. Add ½ of the blueberries, lemon juice, vanilla and almond extracts, and fold together with flour and sugar.
4. Roll piecrust into a circle and put into an 8″ pie pan.
5. Pour mixture into piecrust.
6. Add remaining blueberries and spread evenly to edges.
7. Encircle tart with strawberries as shown and dot top with butter.
8. Bake for 30–40 minutes.
9. Serve warm or at room temperature.

This unexpected use of my American folk art wagon adds to our summer fun. It creates a special presentation for these colorful lobsters. Nestled in a bed of cracked ice and lemon wedges, these summer treats make for a glorious lunch. Look around your own house and experiment with inventive ways to use your decorative collections for fun and surprises.

A Festive Evening

Our area in the Northeast is known worldwide for its lobster. Lobsters beside the pool over beds of ice, served with lemon wedges and any of the 7 sauces, page 56, make a grand brunch.

For a gala, a decorative column has been topped with a head of fresh greens. The lettuce head was simply washed and unfolded on top of the pedestal, then lobsters were arranged on top of this nest of green. Garnished with wedges of lemon, this dramatic presentation spices the festive table. Nutcrackers from any hardware store can be used to open the lobster shells.

NEW ENGLAND BOILED LOBSTER

Ingredients:
Water to cover
1–1½ pounds live lobster per person

1. Bring water to hard boil in large pot.
2. Add each live lobster and boil for 5 minutes.
3. Reduce heat to simmer. Cook for an additional 15 minutes.
4. Drain and serve immediately for a hot lobster dinner or refrigerate to serve for a cold brunch or lunch dish.

MIDSUMMER'S MENU

Americana Salad
New England Lobster
Sweet Corn
Kashmir Cream

AMERICANA SALAD

Serves 6–8

Ingredients:
2 heads red leaf lettuce
2 bunches flat leaf spinach
2 pints cherry tomatoes
1 medium Spanish (purple) onion

1. Wash and clean greens. Drain and dry.
2. Wash cherry tomatoes. Drain and dry.
3. Peel and slice onion.
4. Arrange in large salad bowl.
5. Serve with Oregano Dressing.

OREGANO DRESSING

Ingredients:
3 teaspoons dried oregano
1 clove garlic, peeled and finely chopped
½ cup olive oil
¼ cup balsamic vinegar
1 tablespoon cracked black pepper
1 teaspoon salt

1. Combine all ingredients.
2. Pour over salad and toss to coat greens.

Sweet Corn

resh corn is appearing in our markets earlier and earlier each year. This year, the first of the season's corn was available on the Fourth of July. There are many ways to prepare this American favorite, and it takes only a few minutes to prepare in a microwave, in boiling water, or roasted on the grill.

MICROWAVE CORN

Serves 6–8

Ingredients:
1 dozen ears of fresh sweet corn left in the husk

1. Crack husk of corn and run under water so that water envelopes the corn and goes into the leaves of the husk. Fold husk back around corn.
2. Pop into microwave on a glass or ceramic dish and cook at full power for 5–6 minutes. If cooking more than 1–2 ears at a time, increase cooking time and turn ears to steam evenly.

ROASTED CORN

Serves 6–8

Ingredients:
1 dozen ears fresh sweet corn

1. Crack husk and run under water until husk is soaked and corn is enveloped in water. Fold husk back around corn.
2. Place ears of corn on rack over hot coals. Cook approximately 20–25 minutes, turning ears every 5 minutes or so. A variation is to remove the husk from corn and wrap each ear separately in 1 layer of heavy-duty tinfoil. Drop ears into coals. Turn every 5 minutes until fully cooked.

BOILED CORN

Serves 6–8

Ingredients:
1 dozen ears of fresh sweet corn

1. Remove husk and silk.
2. Bring a large pot of water to a hard boil.
3. Drop corn into water and cook 5–10 minutes depending on the size, age, and amount of corn.
4. Drain and serve.

SWEET BUTTER SAUCE

Serves 6–8

Ingredients:
2 sticks sweet butter
1 tablespoon honey
1 tablespoon cracked black pepper
1 pinch salt

1. Soften butter to room temperature.
2. Knead with fork.
3. Add honey, pepper, and salt.
4. With a spoon, fold mixture together.
5. Serve in country crockery or individual glass cellars beside each plate.

Kashmir Cream

Our favorite dessert is Kashmir Cream. It's the perfect finish for an elegant meal. This dessert becomes a basic foundation that can be dressed up with many different garnishes to fit the drama of the evening. It can be molded into a fantasy by using one of our decorative molds—from the charm and whimsy of a lamb, to the humor of Mickey Mouse, to the simple grace of a glass pie dish. It's amazingly beautiful presented in the center of a classic, white plate. It takes on a visual excitement layered on a repousse silver tray, surrounded by the vibrant red of a raspberry puree.

You can also serve it with fresh sauteed peaches, in season. The contrasts between sensations of the cool, velvety texture of the Kashmir Cream, covered with hot, fresh peaches sauteed in butter and brown sugar, creates a special treat.

A formal presentation centers the servings on oversize service plates at least 12 inches in diameter. For a more casual approach, I placed it in a large wooden vessel that I found on a trip to Marrakesh. Our collection of majolica leaf plates were used. The shell service spoons are treasured utensils from Kashmir, Finland.

KASHMIR CREAM

Ingredients:
2 cups heavy cream
½ cup sugar
small pinch salt
2 envelopes of unflavored gelatin
½ cup warm water
1 pint sour cream
¼ teaspoon vanilla

1. Heat cream, but do not boil.
2. Add sugar and the pinch of salt.
3. Soften gelatin in water and stir to dissolve, while heating cream.
4. Add gelatin and stir to mix thoroughly.
5. Remove from heat and fold in sour cream and vanilla.
6. Butter a 5-cup mold and pour in cream mixture. Refrigerate to chill. For quick set put in freezer for 20 to 30 minutes.
7. Unmold.
Serves 6 to 8.

SWEET GEORGIA BROWN

Ingredients:
6 ripe peaches, peeled
¼ lb sweet butter (1 stick)
½ cup brown sugar

Cut each peach into 8 slices. In a saute pan heat butter until bubbling, but do not burn. Lower heat. Stir in brown sugar. Add peaches and saute until peaches become soft. Serve over Kashmir Cream, ice cream or cake.

LIGHT KASHMIR CREAM

Ingredients:
½ cup boiling water
1 envelope unflavored gelatin
½ teaspoon Sweet & Low®
⅓ cup skim milk powder
½ teaspoon vanilla
8 ice cubes, crushed

Pour water into blender. Sprinkle gelatin on it. Blend to dissolve. Turn off blender. Add all other ingredients except ice cubes and blend. Add crushed ice slowly, blending on high speed for one minute.

Pour into mold. Put in freezer for 5 to 10 minutes. Unmold.

Top with fresh strawberries or blueberries.

FESTIVE TABLES

For

Fall

Harvest

all begins softly. After Labor Day, the color mood changes in New York and the Hamptons. The first red or golden leaves signal the new season, as does the change of produce in the markets. The colors of bright orange, strong golds, and rich greens predominate in the landscape and in the fruits and vegetables. Brilliant pumpkins and golden gourds echo the colors of nature's changing leaves. Overnight, the nurseries are filled with mums in a rich array of burnished gold, antique rose, vibrant burgundies, and burnished rusts. Around the world, the harvest has always been celebrated. Here in America it has become a national day to give thanks for our bounty.

Large crockery filled with changing leaves are so beautiful and signal the coming of fall. Down back roads, the sun is lower on the horizon. Nature's new coat of colors begins to appear in markets.

Our harvest meal under the trees starts with a buffet. An overscaled twig wreath is layered with orange and gold peppers, fall gourds, mushrooms, and kum-quats. Ivy twines with the wreath also as it garlands the table.

Indian Summer

As fall begins, Indian summer reminds us that it will not be long before winter's short, cold days will move our entertaining indoors. For our last event under the trees, I host a harvest buffet. Special decorative plates made from golden doilies are pressed into baskets. These baskets, used as holder for paper plates, are readily available in the summer in most hardware stores. One afternoon I pressed a golden doily into a basket holder and inserted a clear glass plate. It's become a standard service plate for all kinds of occasions.

Materials:
10″ basket paper plate holders
Elmer's Glue
12″ golden paper doilies
paper towel or cloth
colorful fall leaves
10″ clear glass plates

1. Coat basket holder with glue.
2. Center doily over basket and rub into basket with paper towel or cloth. The doily will stretch and conform to the basket shape. Let dry.
3. Place a colorful fall leaf, flower, or a piece of Victorian scrap memorabilia in center of doily.
4. Center glass plate on top of the decoration as shown for a memorable lunch plate.

RUM CIDER

Serves 1

Ingredients:
1 cup fresh or bottled apple cider, fresh preferred
¼ cup golden rum, or to taste
1 cinnamon stick

1. Combine all ingredients in saucepan and warm.
2. Serve in a festive mug or goblet using cinnamon stick as stirrer.

A warm mellow drink that is wonderful each fall when the cider is on farm stands is made with fresh cider and captures the essence of fall.

HARVEST MENU

Magic Crudités
Harvest Soup
Patty Pan Peppers
Honey Roasted Chicken

Magic Crudités

Fresh vegetable crudités, sliced and skewered, are a light and elegant beginning to a full dinner. Many of our friends are stressing vegetables more and more in their diets. A light and magical hors d'oeuvre is made of vegetables sprinkled with black sesame seeds. For our harvest meal, while preparations are being made, I set out these small treats on a wonderful terra-cotta or marble charger plate. Individual skewers of crudités have been wrapped in a golden sun collar. A tapestry table runner protects the table.

Blanching in boiling water is a fine way to enhance the flavor and color of many vegetables. They should remain tender and crisp. Different varieties will require different blanching times. Put each vegetable into cold water after blanching to stop cooking and to chill. Crudités can be served with the seven sauces from page 56.

MAGIC CRUDITÉS

Serves 6–8

Ingredients:
2 cups sugar snap peas, topped and tailed
2 cups sliced red sweet peppers
2 cups sliced yellow peppers
2 cups sliced orange peppers
2 cups asparagus spears
2 cups baby carrots
2 cups snow peas, topped and tailed
½ cup black sesame seeds
2 tablespoons olive oil for each vegetable

1. Blanch sugar snap peas approximately 1 minute.
2. Blanch different peppers separately, for approximately 2–3 minutes.
3. Blanch asparagus spears approximately 3–5 minutes depending on stalk size.
4. Blanch baby carrots approximately 3 minutes.
5. Blanch snow peas approximately 30 seconds.
6. Set all vegetables aside.
7. In dry pan quickly toast sesame seeds over high heat.
8. Add seeds to oil and toss with vegetables.

Harvest Soup

When Indian summer brings us outdoors for one last festive party, I set our table under the trees with a cornucopia of harvest decorations from our local farm stand. Overscaled crockery that has been used throughout the year inside our home is encircled with a vegetable laden wreath. For party events, the wreath creates a perfect frame for this autumn harvest.

A HARVEST WREATH

Materials:

orange and yellow peppers, fall squash, green apples, kumquats, mushrooms

twig wreath

florist wire

ivy

1. Place the medley of fruits and vegetables around the wreath as shown. Work with your color placement to balance the cascade of color from greens to yellows to orange. Florist wire can be used as needed to hold position of elements.
2. Intertwine ivy between decorative elements to create an interlacing element.

TOMATO SOUP

Serves 8–10

Ingredients:

2 cups fresh or canned tomatoes, cut up and skinned

½ cup chopped celery

¼ cup chopped onions

2 teaspoons brown or white sugar

2 tablespoons sweet butter

2 tablespoons flour

1 cup milk

¼ cup chopped onion

½ small bay leaf

sour cream

mint leaves

1. Place tomatoes, celery, onions, and sugar in a pot and simmer, covered, for about 15 minutes.
2. Melt butter over a low heat.
3. Blend in 1½–2 tablespoons flour over low heat for 3–5 minutes.
4. Add milk slowly and stir.
5. Add onion and bay leaf.
6. Cook and stir until thickened and smooth.
7. Strain into the tomato and vegetable stock.
8. Serve hot or chilled. If served chilled, garnish with spiral of sour cream and mint as shown.

I love anything oversized. Especially large plates. Food always looks better when framed with overscaled service pieces. I also like to play with everyday vegetables. I bring home big bags of produce and use the vegetables as decorative elements instead of hiding them away. After the day's events, they are refrigerated and used in a later meal. It's all a part of the joy of the unexpected and entertaining.

Patty Pan Peppers

Red, yellow, and orange peppers are festive additions to any event. Their sweet flavor and lively quality add a special vibrancy to many a table. Relatively new to our American palate, these are dressed-up versions of our old friend the green bell pepper. With the addition of patty pan squash and baby asparagus, this makes an unusual hors d'oeuvre or vegetable side dish for a buffet.

SAUTEED PEPPERS, PATTY PAN SQUASH, AND BABY ASPARAGUS

Serves 8–10

Ingredients:
24 stalks baby asparagus
18 patty pan squash, assorted sizes
2 red peppers
2 yellow peppers
2 orange peppers
¼ cup olive oil
2 cloves garlic, peeled and sliced
1 tablespoon oregano
¼ teaspoon sugar
salt and cracked whole pepper to taste

1. Blanch asparagus and squash to soften. Remove from water and set aside.
2. Cut peppers in half, trim, and remove seeds.
3. Cut peppers into ¼" slices. Set aside.
4. In a heavy iron skillet, heat oil over medium heat.
5. Sauté garlic and peppers until soft.
6. Add asparagus and squash. Stir until heated.
7. Add oregano, sugar, and salt and pepper to taste.
8. Serve immediately.

For a fall evening, a mood of warmth was created by using a service platter in russet tones. A table runner was created out of an Oriental carpet. Candlelight from eastern European candlesticks of repoussé brass sheds a warm glow over the table. Skewers encircled with a golden sun napkin ring are placed beside the platter for easy use. Stacks of small terracotta plates are used to repeat the color theme. Cascades of golden dried hydrangea are placed all over the table.

Honey Roasted Chicken

Rich in flavor and aroma, my roasted chicken is nestled on a bed of sautéed Spanish onions and pecans and served in eighteenth-century English soup bowls. This tapestry of flavors is encircled by eighteenth-century Russian candlesticks. I decorated our table with a garden of golden dried hydrangea and exotic brass and wooden lions.

HONEY ROASTED CHICKEN ON A BED OF ONIONS AND NUTS

Serves 8–10
Ingredients:
¼ frying chicken per person
½ cup honey
salt
2 tablespoons freshly cracked black pepper

1. Preheat over to 450°.
2. Coat chicken with honey on both sides.
3. Lightly salt chicken on both sides.
4. Place chicken in roasting pan, skin side up.
5. Sprinkle with cracked pepper.
6. Reduce oven heat to 350° and cook 45 minutes, basting with honey every 15 minutes.
7. Serve on bed of sautéed Spanish (purple) onions and pecans.

HONEY NUT AND ONION SAUTE

Ingredients:
½ stick sweet butter
3 large Spanish (purple) onions, peeled and coarsely chopped
3 cups pecans, shelled
salt to taste
½ cup honey

1. Melt butter in large skillet.
2. Sauté onions until soft.
3. Add pecans and stir-fry slowly until they become golden and crispy brown. Remove from heat and lightly salt.
4. Add honey and mix.
5. Turn out on large platter. Arrange chicken on this sweet bed.
6. Since I had a few extra red peppers left over from Patty Pan Peppers, I added them as a garnish.

Manhattan Nights

At the beginning of October, Indian summer is over and our energy is centered in our Manhattan home. The air is crisp. New plays are opening. My design life returns to full intensity.

Nancy and I believe a home does not come alive until it is dressed with personal style. Our search throughout the flea markets and antique fairs is an important part of our lives. We not only use our collections of various objects to decorate our tables, they're also an inspiration for my design work. A duck decoy may become a centerpiece. A sphere on a pedestal today may be tossed in an urn tomorrow or be found sitting on a candlestick as part of a buffet display next week. These beloved objects are used. So many people have beautiful homes full of glorious objects that are only seen. What a waste! It is so much more exciting to make your collectibles an integral part of your entertaining style.

We all used to think of business dinners as staid, stiff occasions. A client of mine asked me to give a dinner after showing my line of ceramics last fall. He warned that the business guests were conservative people from the South and that the mood of the evening would be reserved. The guest list ended up with twenty-five names, not a small dinner. Being Southerners, Nancy and I knew that even the most conservative guest loves to have a good time. To break the ice, and to create a lighthearted fantasy evening, I set a place for each person with a different Victorian mask.

To avoid social gaffes, and to create a relaxed feeling, seat selection was by lottery. Each place setting had a number. Before each course, each person had to select a number and act out the role of their mask. Vice presidents became chambermaids, buyers became captains of the Scottish Guard. The exuberant mood created by this catalytic device enveloped the room and set the scene for a cordial business relationship.

Halloween Masquerade

Halloween is a holiday of fantasy and magic. A decade ago, in Greenwich Village, a small local parade started that has grown to a major citywide event. Costumed people parading around the square has crescendoed into New York's version of New Orleans's Mardi Gras or Rio's Carnival. A few years ago we lived on Ninth Street off Fifth Avenue in the center of this frivolity. Friends started dropping in after the parade, and we served them drinks. It was great fun. Over the years, our Halloween party has become a major night and a much-anticipated event. The past few years, I have set themes for costumes and decorations. Friends have rallied around these party themes with wholehearted invention.

1992
The Russian Revolutions
The color was red, naturally.

1991
Voguing in Venice
The color was gold.

1990
BooBoo Baroque!
The resurgence of the baroque style began, and our invitations signaled the color also was gold.

1989
Leopard Safari.
Leopard print was decreed as an essential element in all costumes.

Russian Revolutions

*N*ot a historical event, the Russian Revolution is fertile ground for a masquerade. There are so many characters and historical periods to ignite the imagination. One example is the revolution of Catherine the Great, from the film *The Scarlet Empress*, directed by Josef Von Sternberg. This unique period and film create images of lush imperial palaces, handsome military uniforms, a style of mysterious grandeur. The revolution of 1917 creates visions of Lenin, Stalin, and severe austerity. Today, the new revolution invites political satire, starring Gorbachev and Yeltsin.

For my decorative theatrics, of course, I chose the lush soul of an imperial masquerade. We set our Halloween table for the arrival of the revelers.

A garden sculpture of a seventeenth-century nobleman became the center of our buffet masquerade. Over 100 guests would be parading through during the night. The mood was lush, but the food and service ware were not costly.

108

Boom! Boom!

Friends returning from Carnaval in Rio brought back a national treasure, the Brazilian national drink, Caipirinha, which puts Rio in a party mood. Our version of this is sure to bless every party with a festive mood. Boom!Boom! has the sweet taste of an innocent limeade, with the kick of Finnish vodka.

I use my elegant coffee urn for many casual functions. In bygone days, this nineteenth-century coffee samovar was to-the-manner born. I use this wonderful piece for punch, gin, and tonics, grog, and Boom! Boom!

BOOM! BOOM!
Serves 1

Ingredients:
1 lime, sliced in half wedges as shown
3 jiggers vodka
3 tablespoons granulated sugar
cracked ice

Serves 20

20 limes, sliced in half wedges, as shown
1.75 litre bottle vodka
2 cups granulated sugar
cracked ice

1. Squeeze juices from lime into container.
2. Drop lime sections into glass, punch bowl, or samovar. Cover with sugar, pound, and mix.
3. Cover with vodka and stir vigorously.
4. Serve with a generous amount of lime chunks and cracked ice.

At large gatherings like Halloween, I fill enormous baskets with decorative fruits and gold and silver plastic tumblers. The practical yet elegant tumblers can be saved from party to party. Votive candles glow before an antique mirror.

Our Hero

In this season, Nancy's and my business life is furiously active. With a large gathering of people coming, we never have time to make hors d'oeuvres. A simple solution with a spectacular effect is to call the local deli or hero shop and have them deliver an overscaled hero sandwich that can be sliced into bite-sized pieces and served as finger food. This solution has always been a crowd pleaser and something that allows us to see friends or make our home available for an event at times when our lives are particularly stressful. Everyone has a favorite local deli and, most often, they will prepare "Super heros." A party handled in such a simple manner and with your friends all pitching in and bringing their own drinks to share on a spur of the moment for Halloween, after football games, or any weekend night can be an instant success.

Years ago, at a friend's fine East Side townhouse, a group of us were having cocktails and great conversation. Suddenly, oversized baskets of Big Macs® in silver foil tied in ribbons arrived, an easy, humorous, and great way to thrown an instant dinner party.

112

Bittersweet berries gathered and arranged among our collection of folk art ceramics is an example of simple and instant decorating magic. This lovely apothecary cabinet is from a shop in Quogue, Long Island. It houses our collection of flatware, an unexpected silver chest.

Thanksgiving Gathering

At Thanksgiving in our house, our friends arrive in late afternoon. The sun is low in the sky and casts its golden glow across the scene. The table setting has been created to enhance our harvest meal. The table has been dressed with gilded fruit and miniature pumpkins. Napkins have been folded into fox head stirrup cups, traditional drinking vessels that in our forefathers' days were filled with spirits and used before the hunt to give courage. Most often found in silver, these humorous ceramic versions are twentieth-century reproductions.

Our Thanksgiving menu is, like Christmas, an event that requires more than our usual preparation. So that we are not hectic on the day itself, most of this menu is prepared the night before and refrigerated. It only has to put in the oven to be cooked. We can enjoy time with our friends all Thanksgiving Day.

THANKSGIVING MENU

Pumpkin Nutmeg Soup
Roasted Thanksgiving Turkey
Sautéed Peppers
Candied Cranberries
Mrs. Appleyard's Corn Bread Dressing
with Pecans and Fruit
Candied Sweet Potatoes
in Orange Baskets
Cinnamon Walnut Pound Cake

Fall Splendor

Fall, with its outpouring of readily available fruit and flora, is a time when seasonal arrangements can lavish atmosphere on social gatherings. Our woodlands are ready for harvest. Leaves, flowers, and berries in an endless array bring these deep, rich harvest colors into your home. A large basket with a gathering of leaves simply tossed into place can have a spectacular effect. Seasonal dried flowers and leaves mixed with fresh vegetables and gilded fruits form arrangements with baroque magnificence.

Materials:
1 large basket
florist wire
1 candlestick for height
collection of leaves
dried hydrangea
bittersweet berries

1. Wire basket to base of candlestick.
2. Group the collection of leaves in the basket in a bouquet. Because of the height of your basket, be sure your collection is balanced not only for visual effect, but so that this topiary of leaves is on solid foundation.
3. Put dried hydrangea into place throughout arrangement.
4. To create cascade effect, use bittersweet to one side to create a grand flourish.

The center of our harvest table is the arrangement of leaves from Halloween. I added a cornucopia of gilded fruit and miniature pumpkins to underline the harvest theme. Candlesticks act as holders for gilded pineapples, a traditional symbol of welcome.

Pumpkin Tureen

Nothing starts a Thanksgiving meal with a more glorious flourish than when I serve one of Nancy's rich soups in a tureen made from a pumpkin and surrounded by an array of decorative cabbage and flowers. This festive arrangement begins our annual feast. Candlesticks hold pineapples to welcome friends.

PUMPKIN NUTMEG SOUP

Serves 8–10

Ingredients:
6 cups canned pumpkin
6 cups half-and-half
½ stick butter
5 tablespoons brown sugar
¼ teaspoon salt
2 teaspoons ground nutmeg
chopped pecans for garnish

1. Put all ingredients except 1 teaspoon nutmeg and pecans in a blender. Blend until smooth.
2. Heat over medium heat. Do not boil.
3. Pour in tureen of pumpkin.
4. Garnish with 1 teaspoon nutmeg and pecans.
5. Serve.

Soup can be stored in a warm oven for a short while, if desired, while waiting to serve.

Pumpkin Tureen
Materials:
4 decorative cabbages
large tray
8″–10″ round cake pan
medium-sized pumpkin, topped and cleaned
small bunch of variegated miniature chrysanthemums
warmer candles

1. Unpot decorative cabbages leaving roots on.
2. Arrange on a large tray so roots overlap and create a cross.
3. Turn cake pan upside down on cross to create stand for pumpkin.
4. Position pumpkin in cake pan. The weight of the pumpkin will hold the cabbages in place.
5. Position leaves of cabbage close to pumpkin to cover the base. Dot with chrysanthemums, or other flowers or berries, as decoration.
6. Circle presentation with lit warmer candles for a spectacular effect.

Sweet Potato Baskets

This Southern tradition uses orange halves as service baskets for sweet potatoes. Dressed up with whole pecans and toasted marshmallows, they are beautiful as well as full of rich, sweet taste. These silver holders, from an elegant cream soup bowl service, are perfect to present our orange baskets at special times. A tower of treats has been created by using our golden service plates and silver tumblers stacked like a medieval tower.

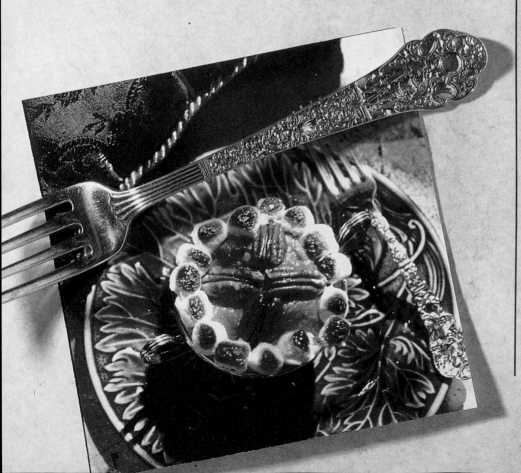

CANDIED SWEET POTATOES IN ORANGE BASKETS

Serves 8–10

Ingredients:
12 large sweet potatoes
1 pound butter
1 cup brown sugar
1½ cups chopped pecans
teaspoon salt
orange halves, cleaned
whole pecans for garnish
marshmallows

1. Wash sweet potatoes and put into large pot of boiling water.
2. Boil for 30 minutes until skin breaks away and potatoes are soft.
3. Allow potatoes to sit for 10–15 minutes. While they are still warm, remove skins.
4. Mix potatoes, brown sugar, chopped pecans, and salt in a large bowl.
5. Put into orange halves. Refrigerate.
6. Preheat oven to 350° and cook for 30 minutes.
7. Garnish with pecans and marshmallows.
8. Return to oven until brown.

Thanksgiving Harvest

ROASTED THANKSGIVING TURKEY

Serves 8–10

Ingredients:
20-pound turkey, giblets removed
melted butter
poultry seasoning
oregano
salt
pepper

1. Preheat oven to 425°.
2. Brush turkey with melted butter.
3. Sprinkle inside and out with poultry seasoning, oregano, salt, and pepper.
4. Put turkey on poultry rack in bottom of large roasting pan.
5. Roast turkey for 10 minutes.
6. Lower heat to 350°. Roast for 20 minutes per pound.
7. Baste every 20 minutes until turkey is done. Check that juices run clear and the drumstick moves easily.

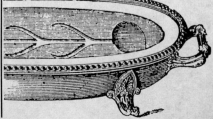

SWEET PEPPERS WITH SAUTEED CRANBERRIES

Serves 8–10

Ingredients:
5–6 large green sweet peppers
2 large yellow peppers
1 large red sweet pepper
¼ cup olive oil
½ cup sun-dried cranberries
1 tablespoon sugar
1 tablespoon cracked black pepper
pinch of salt

1. Cut all peppers in slivers. Set red pepper aside.
2. Sauté green and yellow peppers in olive oil for 3–5 minutes or until soft.
3. Add cranberries, sugar, black pepper and salt and sauté until cranberries soften.
4. Serve garnished with uncooked red peppers.

CANDIED CRANBERRIES

Serves 8–10

Ingredients:
1 package fresh cranberries
¾ cup water
1½ cups sugar
juice of 2 large oranges, ½ cup
⅛ teaspoon cream of tartar

1. Bring all ingredients to a boil.
2. Stir until berries begin to pop open and sugar saturates berries.

CRANBERRY ORANGE SAUCE

Serves 8–10

Ingredients:
To the above ingredients, add
pulp from 2 oranges
1 orange rind cut into small slivers
½ cup chopped pecans
1 teaspoon cinnamon

1. Put all ingredients in a pan and simmer for 1 hour.
2. Refrigerate.

The Thanksgiving turkey is an American family tradition. Nothing tastes better or is easier to prepare than this familiar favorite. Fresh turkeys are always better. Usually you can find them in the markets. Even if you have to order one in advance from your butcher, the taste is worth it. I always make enough to have lots of leftovers.

Family Dressing

When I remember our Thanksgiving in the Old South, I recall our mother's corn bread dressing. It was never the Appleyard's family tradition to serve stuffing in the bird. She always believed that would be too dry. Her basic recipe is prepared and served as a pudding in a casserole dish. I have experimented with it and done variations from year to year. The basic bread stuffing can be augmented with a range of flavorings to create your own family tradition. For different holidays, the shifting tastes can be changed by varying the fruits, nuts or sausage, mushrooms, and spices to create totally different flavors.

MRS. APPLEYARD'S CORN BREAD DRESSING

Basic recipe
Serves 8–10

Ingredients:
1 stick butter
2 large white onions, peeled and coarsely chopped
1 bunch celery, cleaned and coarsely chopped
1 16-ounce package Pepperidge Farm Herb Seasoned Stuffing
1 tablespoon freshly cracked pepper
3 tablespoons Bell's Seasoning
10 cups of stale corn bread
1 cup turkey drippings
1 cup milk
1 cup water
3 cups chicken or turkey broth

For a sweet fruit flavor, add 3 cups mixed dried fruits and 2 cups chopped pecans, coarsely cut.

1. Preheat oven to 350°.
2. Melt butter in large pan and sauté onions and celery until soft.
3. Add Pepperidge Farm Stuffing and all other ingredients and combine thoroughly. Mixture should be the consistency of a soft pudding. If dry, add more chicken or turkey broth. Put into large, flat decorative casserole dish that can be used to serve. I love my terra-cotta oven-to-table cookware. This can be stored in the refrigerator until ready to cook.
4. Cook for 45 minutes or until firm and brown on top. Decorate top 15 minutes before finish time with dried fruits, apricots, prunes, and whole pecans.

For my buffet presentation, I surrounded a terra-cotta casserole with a twig wreath and garnished this Thanksgiving tradition with miniature pumpkins and broccoli.

Celebration Cake

To end our Thanksgiving celebration, Nancy prepares a cake I always look forward to serving. It is made with sour cream and has the consistency of a dense pound cake. I love nuts and this cake has a delicious nutty topping.

An elegant cake pedestal was created simply by turning over a silver tumbler and placing the cake plate on top. Be sure the base of the tumbler is wide enough to create a stable foundation.

CINNAMON WALNUT CAKE

Serves 8–10

Ingredients:
2 sticks sweet butter, room temperature
2 cups granulated sugar
4 medium eggs, beaten
2 teaspoons vanilla
2 teaspoons baking powder
2 teaspoons baking soda
4 cups flour
1 pint sour cream

1. Preheat oven to 325°.
2. Cream butter and sugar until fluffy.
3. Add eggs and vanilla.
4. Add alternately 1 teaspoon baking powder, 1 teaspoon baking soda, 2 cups flour, and ½ pint sour cream. Mix well.
5. Add last half of ingredients. Mix well. If batter is too stiff, add a few drops of milk.

CRUST AND FILLING

Ingredients:
1 cup walnuts, chopped
½ cup granulated sugar
3 teaspoons ground cinnamon
butter for pan

1. Mix together all ingredients.

To bake:
1. Butter inside of 10″ Bundt pan.
2. Add half of cake batter to pan.
3. Add half of nut mixture to cover batter.
4. Add remaining batter.
5. Top with remaining nut mixture.
6. Bake for 1–1¼ hours or until toothpick inserted comes out clean.
7. Remove cake from pan to large tray.
8. Invert cake so that nut mixture on cake top falls into tray.
9. Put cake on cake plate and garnish with nut mixture in tray.

I decorated the cake this year with a cascade of golden grapes and gilded acorns.

FESTIVE TABLES

For Winter Fantasies

Recipes, Menus, and Tablesettings for Every Occasion

New York is the quintessential Christmas City. It is alive with color, crisp air and shop windows filled with Christmas fantasies. The Macy's Thanksgiving parade and the decorating of the Christmas tree in Rockefeller Center herald the beginning of the season. Evergreens stream down Park Avenue covered in a twilight of white light. In Central Park, Tavern on the Green wraps the surrounding forest of trees in tiny white stars of light.

Above the corner of Fifth Avenue and Fifty-seventh Street a gigantic luminous snowflake floats. The Christmas fantasies in the windows of Lord & Taylor and Saks draw lines of holiday shoppers.

This annual visual feast has become a family tradition to share with children and creates golden memories for New Yorkers as well as their guests from generation to generation.

CHRISTMAS DINNER MENU

Nancy's Creamed Carrot Soup
Honey Oatmeal Crackers
Christmas Crown Roast of Lamb
Baby Squabs Stuffed with Apricot, Plum, and Corn Bread Dressing
Raymond's Sautéed Mushrooms
Mrs. Appleyards' Hot and Spicy Corn Bread Dressing
Old South Holiday Ambrosia

Holiday Topiaries

At Christmas, our faux ficus trees take center stage. I would love our New York home to be full of green throughout the year, but it is not as light as our home in the Hamptons. With our travel schedule, it is almost impossible for us to keep plants alive in New York, so we improvise. The floral markets have a wonderful variety of faux plants and trees. They look so real, that even the most discerning eye finds it difficult to detect the faux from the alive.

I dress these unexpected Christmas trees with a spectacular array of holiday ornaments. A few years ago, I splurged on some very special gold Christmas angels from the Ballard Catalog. These beautiful angels are normally considered "tree toppers," but I use them in different ways all year long. Here, they float in the trees. If you have light and real trees, so much the better.

Materials:
8-foot ficus tree, faux or real

6 yards boxwood garland from florist
5–8 yards gold lamé fabric
florist wire
4 angels
6 yards decorative ribbon
6 gilded fruits
4 dried sunflower blossoms
12 pinecones
6 red balls wrapped in ribbon
12–15 poinsettia blossoms

1. Garland Christmas tree with boxwood by encircling trunk as shown.
2. Crush gold lamé into tight ball to create antique-like crinkle. Thread golden garland of lamé throughout tree. Swag the lamé loosely as shown to create ball effect of a topiary. The gold lamé creates the traditional topiary form.
3. With florist wire, attach angels in two groups to create effect of heralding chorus.
4. Wrap ribbon around boxwood garland.
5. With florist wire attach a cornucopia of fruit, flora, pinecones, and red balls as shown.
6. Put one poinsettia blossom in each vial (page 138). Position blossoms throughout tree to create a balance of color.

Christmas Settings

Through the fall, the decorations in our home have been slowly changing from the dried garlands of Halloween, to the fantasies of Thanksgiving's harvest themes, and, finally, to Christmas, when my decorating activities come into full baroque splendor. Our home is bustling and our calendar is full of holiday events.

Nancy and I have created a tradition of two festive gatherings each year. On every December 19, our wedding anniversary, we give a potluck supper in New York style. Black-tie and gala gowns are requested, and each guest is asked to prepare and bring their favorite dish. This way, we create an open house and have our year's largest celebration. As many as 100 guests have joined us in celebrating this joyful night. Centerpieces on a holiday table create and set the mood for the evening. I favor either very low arrangements or extremely tall displays, because the guests' view and conversation should never be restricted.

Greeting each guest this year was a Christmas variation on my pressed flower decorative plates (page 92). First the place was set with golden doilies, on our large golden charger plates. Then I pressed an individual poinsettia blossom behind a clear glass dinner plate. You can insert all kinds of charming objects between the plate and the charger. Christmas cards, antique Victorian images, and family photographs of Christmases past are just a few that come to mind. On the center of the table are Victorian glass ornaments of birds and fruit combined with poinsettias and golden suns.

Red damask napkins have been ringed with gilded wreaths.

Christmas Splendor

Our glorious Christmas table is the essence of the holiday. On Christmas Eve our home is filled with the sound of traditional Christmas carols and the full-bodied aroma of cranberries mixed with Christmas spices. We deck our halls with gold and red and rose. For the last few years, garlands of gold lamé fabric have draped our tables and floated through our trees. This year, the centerpiece was created by simply wiring a gilded basket onto [...] Nancy's carrot soup.

an overscaled baroque candlestick that I decked with Christmas angels, gilded pineapples, and poinsettias of red and rose. At the base a spruce wreath, four feet in diameter, was decorated with a golden sun and rose poinsettias. For fun, I tucked the gilded flatware at each place setting into the wreath. Folded Christmas napkins of red damask were dressed with rings of golden suns, gilded wreaths, and silver soup spoons awaiting the first [...] Nancy's carrot soup.

Materials:
1 large spruce wreath
rose poinsettia blossoms, enough to circle wreath
floral plastic vials filled with water for individual blossoms
florist wire
gilded fruit
Christmas glass fruit and birds
golden sun napkin rings or other decorative objects
golden ribbon
silver flatware

1. Place wreath in center of table.
2. Insert poinsettia blossoms into vials. Cut poinsettia stems on diagonal and scrape with knife so blossom gets as much water as possible. Poinsettias prepared this way should last approximately 7 days, through New Year's Eve. The few that wilt can be replaced with fresh ones.
3. With florist wire, position gilded fruit and Christmas ornaments around wreath.
4. Scatter birds, golden suns, golden ribbon, or other festive, decorative objects around wreath.
5. If desired, tuck flatware into wreath.

Welcome Beginnings

To begin our Christmas Eve dinner, Nancy's soups have become a tradition. This one, a rich blend of carrots, pureed into a warm velvet texture, heralded the beginning of this year's repast. Cream soup bowls, a family heirloom, are served buffet style and set on the gold charger plates. Each serving was garnished with a sunburst of sour cream and freshly ground nutmeg.

NANCY'S GOLDEN CARROT SOUP

Serves 8–10

Ingredients:
1 stick of butter
2 white onions, peeled and chopped
8 large carrots, peeled and sliced
2 stalks celery, chopped
2, 16-ounce cans chicken broth
4, 1-pint containers half-and-half
salt and pepper to taste
½ teaspoon ground nutmeg
nutmeg and sour cream for garnish

1. Melt butter in 6–8-quart pot. Add onions, carrots, and celery. Cook over low heat 10 minutes until soft. Stir often.
2. Add broth. Stir. Cook for 10 minutes.
3. Puree onions, carrots, and celery in food processor or blender. Add 2 pints half-and-half. Blend. Return to pot.
4. Add remaining half-and-half, salt, pepper, and ½ teaspoon nutmeg. Mix well.
5. Heat, do not boil.
6. Serve as shown, garnished with sour cream and nutmeg.

Serve with Honey-Oatmeal Crackers.

HONEY-OATMEAL CRACKERS

Serves 8–10

Ingredients:
¾ cup uncooked oatmeal
¾ cup light brown sugar
1 tablespoon flour
¼ teaspoon salt
½ cup butter, melted
1 egg, beaten
½ teaspoon vanilla

1. Preheat oven to 350°.
2. In a large bowl mix oatmeal, brown sugar, flour, and salt.
3. Stir in melted butter.
4. Add egg and vanilla.
5. On an ungreased cookie sheet, drop half teaspoonfuls of batter two inches apart.
6. Bake 5 minutes or just until brown.
7. Allow to cool, then remove with spatula.

For a robust, sweet cracker to serve with holiday soups, I like this festive crisp. It adds a rich flavor and contrasting texture to our velvety soup course.

Merry Mushrooms

For such a rich meal, a side dish of mushrooms is a nutritious and low-calorie treat. Sautéed and garnished with steamed asparagus, sautéed onions, and chopped eggs, this is a robust yet light accompaniment to our Christmas Crown Roast.

RAYMOND'S SAUTEED PORTOBELLO MUSHROOMS

Serves 8–10

Ingredients:
¼ cup olive oil
4 onions, peeled and coarsely chopped
2 lbs. whole large Portobello mushroom caps (20–30 according to size), stemmed and cleaned
40 spears steamed asparagus, cut into 1½" pieces
6 hard-boiled eggs, peeled and chopped

1. In a 12"–14" skillet, heat oil. Sauté onions until soft.
2. Sauté mushrooms on each side.
3. Add steamed asparagus and remove from heat.
4. Garnish with chopped egg.

Squabs, Cornish hens or even wild game, like quail, are nutritious additions when serving a festive meal of roasted lamb. Some of our friends prefer fowl to red meat and this combination suits most tastes. Squab can be ordered from most specialty butchers, either with or without bones. These small boned fowl are particularly well-suited for stuffing, as it helps retain the bird's original form. They become tiny treats that are easy to handle.

ROASTED GAME WITH FRUIT DRESSING

Serves 8–10

Ingredients:
1 squab per person
½ stick melted butter
a pinch of Bell's Poultry Seasoning per bird
a pinch of salt and cracked black pepper per bird
1 dried apricot per bird
1–2 tablespoons Mrs. Appleyard's Cornbread Dressing per bird (page 126).

1. Preheat oven to 450°.
2. Brush fowl with melted butter inside and out.
3. Sprinkle lightly inside and out with Bell's Poultry Seasoning, salt and pepper.
4. Place apricot in roof of breast cavity and pack cornbread dressing underneath it.
5. Butter a flat roasting pan with remaining butter.
6. Place birds in pan, breast side up.
7. Roast birds in oven for 5 minutes then reduce heat to 350° and cook for 45 minutes or until tender, depending on size of bird.
8. Serve alone or as a garnish for Christmas Crown Roast.

The Christmas buffet is a glow of candlelight. Our crown roast has been filled with steamed broccoli garnished with sliced red peppers and topped with a stuffed baby squab. Squabs have been placed around the edges of the tray and garnished with broccoli and peppers. Votive candles encircle it and create a spectacular Christmas glow.

Christmas Crown

A Crown Roast is a wonderful change from the traditional Christmas turkey. As easy to prepare as turkey, this more unusual treat always adds special excitement to festive meals. Crown roasts are usually prepared by the butcher from lamb or pork. Most butchers will supply you with the decorative frilled covers for rib ends.

CHRISTMAS CROWN ROAST OF LAMB

Serves 8–10

Ingredients:
1 crown roast of lamb or pork, 2 ribs per person
aluminium foil to wrap rib tips to keep from burning.
1 clove garlic, peeled and cut in half
freshly cracked black pepper to taste
oregano, enough to cover roast
salt to taste

1. Preheat oven to 450°.
2. Cover rib ends with foil to protect from burning.
3. Rub cut halves of garlic clove over roast. Sprinkle with pepper and oregano.
4. Roast for 10 minutes to seal in juices.
5. Reduce heat to 350° and roast 30 minutes to the pound. (For pork, roast 45 minutes to the pound.)
6. Remove from oven when cooked to the way you like it best—rare, medium, or well done.
7. Sprinkle lightly with salt if desired.

A tangy, spicy variation on Mrs. Appleyard's Corn Bread Dressing is created by adding sweet and hot Italian sausage. It is a delicious accompaniment to a rich, full-bodied crown roast.

HOT AND SPICY CORN BREAD DRESSING

Serves 8–10
Ingredients:
1 batch Mrs. Appleyard's Corn Bread Dressing, uncooked (page 126)
2 tablespoons olive oil
3 sweet Italian sausages, cut into ½" slices
1 hot Italian sausage, cut into ½" slices
½ pound button mushrooms, cut in half

1. Heat oil in pan. Brown sausages on all sides.
2. Add mushrooms. Sauté.
3. Fold mixture into the basic corn bread dressing, which may be prepared in advance.
4. Cook for 45 minutes until firm and top has browned.
5. Decorate with garnish of steamed broccoli and carrots as shown.

Old South Ambrosia

A dish that Nancy and I serve each Christmas is a fresh, clean mixture of fruits and nuts. This old Southern recipe is a holiday favorite at Christmas and Thanksgiving dinner. Prepare this simple dish the night before so the flavors combine and enrich each other.

OLD SOUTH AMBROSIA

Serves 8–10

Ingredients:
12 navel oranges
4 ounces pecans, whole or chopped
1 7-ounce package shredded coconut

1. Peel and section oranges. Remove all traces of pulp. Navel oranges are larger, sweeter, and more full-bodied than others, and they're seedless. They provide perfect wedges of orange for this visually appealing treat.
2. In a large bowl, combine orange wedges, pecans, and shredded coconut. Refrigerate.
3. Serve cold.

Ambrosia is traditionally served in Southern homes in cut glass bowls. The color is so beautiful and fresh, and the mix of ingredients looks so festive that I serve it in crystal dessert compotes or goblets. I have used a pedestal dessert compote for our buffet presentation and garnished the ambrosia with a festive gold sun.

Welcome Friends

New Year's Eve for us is always a small gathering of close friends. After a season full of festive celebrations, we prefer a quiet time for the close of the year. The traditional hectic celebration of New Year's in large crowds with party hats and noise-makers is not for us; we like to share a wonderful evening at the theater with a few friends. Tickets to the most sought-after shows are easy to get on this night. Most New Yorkers are in a party mood, as are people all over the nation, and we have found that theaters are more apt to have good tickets available. The plays let out early, about ten to ten-thirty. When we get out of the the-ater, we're in the Broadway area. The crowds have begun to gather in Times Square and we get a taste of the growing excitement. We return home, have a light repast, listen to music, and share stories of good times.

For New Year's Eve, our Christmas display is pared down. The blaze of red is removed to leave a soft glow of gold and white with a touch of rose. Urns are decorated throughout our home in a soft glow of rose and gold ready for the New Year's celebration.

Caviar Morsels

Caviar is salted fish roe. The most expensive is Beluga, from Russia or Iran. It is delicious, but obviously only for rare occasions. I like to use caviar more casually, because it tastes wonderful and looks festive, so I buy red and black lumpfish caviar, which is inexpensive and available in most supermarkets.

CAVIAR AND CUCUMBER MORSELS

Serves 6–8
Ingredients:
12 Ritz crackers
12 slices fresh cucumber
3 tablespoons mayonnaise or sour cream
6 tablespoons black or red caviar
½ lemon

1. Place slice of cucumber on each cracker.
2. Spread a bit of mayonnaise or sour cream on cucumber.
3. Top with a teaspoon of caviar and a squeeze of lemon.

This is a wonderful way to use leftover chili, if you have any!

CHILI CRISP

Serves 6–8

Ingredients:
1 cup chili, page 72.
12 leaves lettuce, washed and dried
toothpicks

1. Heat chili.
2. Put 1 teaspoon chili on to each lettuce leaf and make into roll.
3. Secure with toothpick and serve.

POTATO AND CHIVE MORSELS

Serves 6–8

Ingredients:
12 tiny red potatoes, washed and boiled
2 tablespoons mayonnaise
¼ cup chopped fresh chives
cracked whole black pepper, to taste
6 tablespoons caviar

1. Cut potatoes in half and scoop out potato to create potato cups.
2. Mix together potato scoops, mayonnaise, chives, pepper.
3. Fill potato bowls with mixture.
4. Serve caviar in decorative bowl beside potato cups.
Serve on a large platter layered with chives and chopped greens as shown.

Champagne Toast

Champagne, so easy to use throughout the year, is an especially festive way to bring in the New Year. My country crock has been filled with champagne bottles. I used napkin rings in an unexpected way. It was also easy to add a simple bow for a festive touch. The elegant champagne display was wreathed in gilded brown paper and gilded fruit. A charming refresher to add to this classic New Year's libation is a float created by pouring champagne over sorbet.

CHAMPAGNE SORBET

Individual servings

Ingredients:
1 scoop sorbet
champagne to fill glass

1. Spoon sorbet into goblet.
2. Cover with champagne.

This is a wonderful refreshment when made with lemon or orange sorbet. Use your most beautiful champagne goblets.

A perfect accompaniment to a glass of champagne is an anise toast. Mark Rossi shared his mother's recipe with us and it has become part of our holidays.

LIVIA'S ANISE TOAST

Serves 8–10
Ingredients:
1 pat butter
1 tablespoon flour
2 eggs
⅔ cup sugar
1 teaspoon anise seed
1 cup flour
½ teaspoon baking powder
powdered sugar to taste
1 pint strawberries, topped and cleaned

1. Preheat oven to 275°.
2. Grease and flour a loaf pan, 9″ × 5″ × 3″
3. Beat eggs.
4. Add sugar, anise, flour, baking powder. Mix well.
5. Pour into loaf pan.
6. Bake for 20 minutes.
7. Remove from pan cut into ½″ slices.
8. Grease baking sheet and toast slices 5 minutes each side until crisp.
9. Sprinkle on both sides with sugar.
10. Serve with strawberries.

Fire and Ice

When Nancy and I are throwing a birthday event for a friend, usually Nancy prepares his or her favorite cake. A quick alternative when time is short is piles of ice cream topped with a blaze of birthday candles.

This simple homemade ice cream needs no special equipment to prepare. We prepare part of it the night before and add the finishing touches in the morning, so that it is ready to be served for lunch or dinner.

ORANGE ICE CREAM

Serves 6

Ingredients:
2 cups heavy cream
1 cup granulated sugar
1 cup orange juice
2 tablespoons lemon juice
coconut for garnish

1. Scald 1 cup cream and add sugar.
2. Stir continually until dissolved.
3. Remove from heat.
4. Add remaining cream.
5. Pour into bowl that can withstand the changing temperatures.
6. Freeze until firm.
7. In 5–6 hours, or the next morning, fold in juices and return to freezer.
8. Use as ice cream for Fire and Ice or serve in individual goblets and garnish with coconut.

FIRE AND ICE

Serves 8–10

Ingredients:
2 quarts ice cream, your friend's favorite flavor
(In photograph, vanilla has been used.)
2 cups shredded coconut, fresh or packaged
cinnamon for sprinkling
birthday candles
ribbon

1. In a beautiful vessel, use an ice-cream scoop to create a mountain of ice cream.
2. Cover profusely with the shredded coconut.
3. Sprinkle lightly with cinnamon.
4. Cut lengths of ribbon and cascade from peak to base.
5. Dot candles over ice-cream mountain.
6. Light candles and create a memorable evening.

RAYMOND'S HOLIDAY EGGNOG

Serves 24

Ingredients:
12 egg yolks
1 cup sugar
4 cups whole milk
3¼ cups (1 fifth bottle) golden rum
4 cups (2 pints) whipping cream
freshly ground nutmeg

1. Lightly beat egg yolks in bowl with electric beater.
2. Add sugar. Beat until thick.
3. Add milk and rum. Stir thoroughly.
4. Chill at least three hours.
5. Whip cream until stiff.
6. Fold into chilled mixture before serving.
7. Serve in cut glass bowl. Ladle into punch cups or delicate crystal goblets.
8. Garnish each serving with nutmeg.

Index